FROM **ERROR** TO **ETHICS**

Five Essential Lessons from Teaching Clinicians in Trouble

with inspirational quotes from Sir William Osler

DANIEL SOKOL

First published in Great Britain in 2025 by Daniel Sokol
LONDON

ISBN (print): 978-1-0369-1423-3
ISBN (e-book): 978-1-0369-1593-3

To my parents, with love and gratitude

CONTENTS

FOREWORD

by CHARLES S. BRYAN

Heyward Gibbes Distinguished
Professor of Internal Medicine Emeritus
UNIVERSITY OF SOUTH CAROLINA, COLUMBIA (USA)

Daniel Sokol brings to medicine a unique trio of interests and skillsets. As a barrister, he helps clinicians in trouble and represents patients harmed by the medical system. As an ethicist, he teaches, writes, and counsels. As a humanist, he uses history and biography to illuminate the pitfalls and possibilities of medicine as a profession. He excels in all three areas, which in this booklet coalesce around a single theme: the character of the clinician as a determinant of outcomes not only in clinical practice but also in matters of professional discipline. His message is both cautionary and inspirational.

Does character still matter in a medical world grown increasingly impersonal and technology-dependent? Daniel Sokol answers yes, and I agree.[1]

During the 1990s, there was great interest in medical 'professionalism' on both sides of the Atlantic. The American Board of Internal Medicine listed six elements of professionalism and seven signs and symptoms that indicate betrayal of professionalism. The elements of professionalism were altruism, accountability, excellence, honour, integrity, and respect for others. The signs and symptoms of betrayal of professionalism were abuse of power, arrogance, greed, misrepresentation, impairment, lack of conscientiousness, and conflicts of interest.[2] Additions from Daniel Sokol's folders would include dishonesty, criminal activity, and inappropriate use of social media.

All of these elements, in one way or another, fall under the broad rubric of 'character'.

What do we mean by 'character,' and can it be taught? And how does character relate to ethical sophistication?

'Character' can be defined as 'the propensity to do the right thing in difficult circumstances.' As such, it is an integral part of ethics, which involves choosing how best to act in challenging or morally ambiguous circumstances.

Recent work in philosophy underscores the importance

of character ethics (virtue ethics) as a complement to ethical systems based on duty (deontology) or results (consequentialism). Recent work in psychology suggests that virtues and character strengths can be taught, at least to some extent, and can be enhanced by making ethical reflection a lifelong habit.

To amplify, and to reflect on Daniel Sokol's fifth lesson (Medicine is not 'just a job'), I keep returning to the opening words of *Harrison's Principles of Internal Medicine*, first published in 1950, to the effect that the aim of a medical career should be 'an enduring edifice of character.'[3]

Character-building is never complete. The author of the 14th century allegorical poem *Piers Plowman* understood this well. The central character, aptly named 'Will,' and Will's adviser, aptly named 'Conscience,' develop morally as Will assumes increasing responsibilities. The poem ends with Conscience embarking on yet another journey.[4,5]

Character-building begins with humility and acceptance that we are all flawed humans trying to help other flawed humans with flawed science, technology, and moral guidance. The development of character - and of its guardian, conscience - requires active reflection on our difficult decisions that impact the lives of others. These decisions can arise in morally ambiguous circumstances where one must weigh competing virtues, values, priorities, and ethical principles.[1]

Clinicians facing disciplinary action for one or another infraction should find solace in these reflections. As the saying goes, *'There but by the Grace of God go the rest of us.'* We are all vulnerable to temptations and moral lapses. Remedial programs such as those described by Dr Sokol build on the idea that we are all works-in-progress.

William Osler stressed the importance of ideals, while realising their limitations. He told an audience at McGill, his alma mater, 'Not that we all live up to the highest ideals, far from it—we are only men. But we have ideals, which mean much, and they are realizable, which means more.' [6,7]

William Osler stressed the value of 'the silent influence of character on character' gleaned from studying 'the lives of the great and good of the past.'[8] He quoted Plutarch, the ancient Greek philosopher, to the effect that 'character is long-standing habit'.[9] He might have defined character as doing one's best from hour to hour and from day to day, as summed up by his philosophy of 'day-tight compartments.' We might elaborate that character is the essence of a life in which principles inform goals, goals inform actions, and actions are permeated with cheerfulness, energy, humility, and a high sense of purpose steeped in love for fellow humans, expressed as beneficence (active kindness).[10]

By pairing insights from his advocacy for clinicians in trouble with his knowledge of the inspirational writings of Sir William Osler, Daniel Sokol has produced a small gem worthy of every clinician's bedside library.

CHARLES S. BRYAN

M.D., MACP, FRCP (Edin.), FRCP (London)

The University of South Carolina School of Medicine
Columbia, South Carolina, USA

March 2025

REFERENCES

1. Bryan CS, Babelay AM, 'Building Character: A Model for Reflective Practice' (2009) Academic Medicine 84(9): 1283-1288
2. American Board of Internal Medicine, *Project Professionalism* (Philadelphia 1995)
3. Harrison TR, Beeson PB, Thorn GW, Resnik WH, Wintrobe MM. 'Approach to the Patient (Introduction)', in Harrison TR, Beeson PB, Thorn BW, Resnik WH, Wintrobe MM, (eds) *Principles of Internal Medicine* (New York 1950) 1-5
4. Strohm P, *Conscience: A Very Short Introduction* (Oxford 2011) 13-16, 99-100
5. Wood S, *Conscience and the Composition of Piers Plowman* (Oxford 2012) 2, 11-12
6. Osler W, 'Teaching and Thinking: The Two Functions of a Medical School', in *Aequanimitas, With Other Addresses to Medical Students, Nurses and Practitioners of Medicine* (Philadelphia 1932) 115-129
7. Bryan CS, 'Osler's "L'Envoi" Revisited: The Ideal of Idealism' (1999) The Pharos of Alpha Omega Alpha Honor Medical Society 62(2): 27-31
8. Osler W, 'Books and Men', in *Aequanimitas, With Other Addresses to Medical Students, Nurses and Practitioners of Medicine* (Philadelphia 1932) 207-215
9. Osler W, 'A Way of Life', in Hinohara S, and Niki H, (eds) *A Way of Life and Other Addresses with Commentary and Annotations* (North Carolina 2001) 3-18
10. Bryan CS, 'Osler on Character. Epilogue', in Bryan CS, *Osler: Inspirations from a Great Physician* (New York 1997) 217-219

FROM ERROR TO ETHICS

Five Essential Lessons From Teaching Clinicians in Trouble

For over 20 years, I have taught medical ethics to clinicians, first as a graduate student, then as a lecturer, and since 2011 as a barrister. My journey began with Professor Raanan Gillon's renowned intensive course at Imperial College London, which flourished for decades. In 2007, I developed and led my own Applied Clinical Ethics course, also at Imperial, later joined by Dr Paquita de Zulueta as co-director.

Most attendees were ordinary clinicians with an interest in the subject, but a handful were there under different circumstances: they were in trouble with their regulator, employer, or other disciplinary body.

I long had doubts about the value of the courses for these clinicians. Most of the content was of little relevance to their situation. Thus, in 2020, I founded the Centre for Remedial Ethics. Since then, I have been offering one-to-one ethics training for clinicians facing disciplinary action. They are usually referred by their legal advisers or, if students, by their medical schools.

The preparation method is simple: I start by reviewing the paperwork, such as the written complaint, witness statements, investigation reports, and correspondence. I then identify the ethical issues and develop a day-long programme to address them.

The course is held at my home, providing an informal setting that encourages open and frank discussion. When clients attend in person, we have lunch at a local restaurant, where the conversation continues naturally.

The aim is to cultivate insights, what the celebrated judge Hardy Cross Dillard defined as '*the revelation resulting usually from prolonged effort and intermittent brooding by which unfamiliar phenomena are suddenly grasped, or familiar phenomena are suddenly seen in a fresh light.*'[1] However, for the clinicians on my course, insights alone are of limited value if they are not translated into action. They

1 Dillard H, 'On Knowledge, Understanding, Wisdom and Imagination' (1969) The Practical Lawyer 15: 12

must lead to something tangible, be it a compelling reflective statement, a strong showing at a tribunal hearing, the creation of a support network, or changes in habits or behaviour. The stakes are high: careers and livelihoods depend on it.

Over the years, I have worked with hundreds of doctors, dentists, and medical students.

The range of wrongdoing is vast, as reflected by the names of the folders on my computer:

1. Dishonesty
2. Sexual misconduct with a patient
3. Sexual misconduct with a colleague
4. Unprofessional (non-sexual) conduct towards a colleague
5. Domestic violence
6. Other criminal activity (supply of drugs, driving under the influence, failing to pay for train ticket, etc.)
7. Breach of confidentiality/privacy
8. Inappropriate use of social media (e.g., impersonation as another doctor, 'flirting' with a patient)
9. Clinical failures

From this work, I have drawn five key lessons aimed at helping clinicians avoid a fall from grace.

LESSON 1

Make medical ethics education a priority

Few clinicians in my group could remember any ethics teaching from their student days.

Although most medical schools teach their students about the four principles of medical ethics - respect for autonomy, beneficence, non-maleficence and justice - only one attendee at my centre was able to name them all.

Some clinicians, especially international graduates, remember reciting the Hippocratic Oath - or some variant of it - at graduation, but no one could recall any of it.

The Oath features in every course that I deliver. Although dated in parts and restricted in scope, it continues to represent the profound moral commitment of healers towards their patients, even when confronted by temptation. It reminds us that the 'moral nucleus of medical ethics' is the clinical encounter between doctor and patient, that special relationship between one who is ill and one who professes to heal.[2] The Oath says:

> *"And I will use regimens for the benefit of the ill in accordance with my ability and my judgement, but from what is to their harm or injustice I will keep them."*

> *"And in a pure and holy way, I will guard my life and my art."*

The Oath calls for moral vigilance to guard one's integrity, both in the personal and professional spheres. The clinicians on my course have usually dropped their moral guard in some way, violating their Hippocratic duties to do what is best for their patients and the profession.

Sir William Osler (1849-1919), arguably the most influential doctor of modern times, was a great admirer of the Oath. In **Chauvinism in Medicine** (1902), he wrote of 'the high moral ideals, expressed in that most memorable of human documents, the

2 Pellegrino E, *The Philosophy of Medicine Reborn* (Notre Dame 2008) 426

Hippocratic Oath.' In 1910, in an unpublished lecture on **The Lessons of Greek Medicine,** he called the Oath the '*credo*' of the profession. More recently, doctor-ethicist Professor Steven Miles wrote a superb book on the relevance of the Oath to contemporary medicine, concluding that nearly 2500 years after its creation it '*speaks to us still*'.[3]

In October 2024, I visited Hippocrates' birthplace, the small island of Kos, in Greece. Walking around, I saw many statues of the great man and visited the plane tree under which he allegedly taught students. To my wife's bemusement - and a shopkeeper's delight - I bought out a souvenir shop's entire stock of Hippocratic Oaths (English translation), each adorned with a symbolic plane tree leaf, to give to the doctors on my course.

3 Miles S, *The Hippocratic Oath and the Ethics of Medicine* (Oxford 2004)

Statue of Hippocrates in Kos, October 2024

What should we make of the fact that so few clinicians remember anything about the ethics taught at medical school?

In a 2022 survey of medical ethics teachers at UK medical schools, respondents expressed concerns about the low profile of medical ethics and the quality of teaching.[4]

Most of the teaching and assessment of ethics comes at the beginning of a student's medical education, usually in the first two years.[5] This may explain the limited recollection. It would surely be more effective to teach the bulk of the subject in the later years of study and, ideally, during the first few years of clinical work. After all, it is when one begins to practise that the subject truly comes alive.

Many medical students regard ethics as a 'woolly subject', of some philosophical interest but of limited value in the real world of clinical practice. In terms of content, I favour the teaching of medical ethics as a practical discipline. To achieve this, the linkage between ethics and practice must be made clear to students. This does not necessarily require teachers to have a medical degree, but they must have some knowledge of the clinical environment and its pressures.

Clinicians fear the prospect of making clinical errors, which can lead to a legal claim in negligence.

---

4 Deckers J, 'A Survey and Critical Analysis of the Teaching of Medical Ethics in UK Medical School' (2023) International Journal of Ethics Education 8:177-194

5 Devine O *et al*, 'The Analysis of Teaching of Medical Schools Survey' (2020) BMC Medicine 18:126

Much of my work as a barrister deals with these clinical errors, which can be catastrophic for patients but rarely lead to any disciplinary action for the negligent clinician. Ethical mistakes, on the other hand, are more likely to trigger referrals to a local or regulatory authority. They are more likely to result in suspension or erasure from the medical register. It may seem counterintuitive that ethical lapses often attract harsher sanctions than clinical errors that seriously injure patients, but that is the reality, and it reinforces the need for clinicians to have a firm grasp of their ethical obligations.

The vast majority of clinicians on my course have not made clinical errors. They are technically competent. They have made errors of ethics, which may have harmed patients, colleagues, the reputation of the medical profession, and their careers.

Perhaps medical schools should invite these clinicians, whose names are often publicly available in tribunal decisions and the press, to share their experiences with students. I know many who would accept the invitation. They could deliver lessons in ethics more memorably than any textbook or armchair ethicist.

Let me give a simple example. An attendee had been using his elderly father's "free travel" card for his daily work commute. One day, he was stopped at the barrier by an inspector. He was prosecuted for the offence of 'entering a compulsory ticket area without having a valid ticket', convicted in a criminal court, and referred to the regulator. He told me:

> *I thought only healthcare professionals that practise outside their scope or do something insane get in front of their regulator. I never expected that I would end up in this situation. I wish it'd been emphasised to me that, as clinicians, we're held to a higher standard than members of the public.*

That important message, echoed by other clinicians who have attended my courses, will surely resonate louder with students and junior doctors if it came from him than from me.

LESSON 2

Clinicians must recognise their power

About 10% of my cases involve doctors who initiated, or attempted to initiate, a sexual relationship with a current or former patient. In virtually all cases, these relationships are forbidden by ethics and professional rules.

One reason for this is the power imbalance between clinician and patient, and the risk that this brings to the consensual nature of a relationship.

Yet, very few of the clinicians who had breached the rule felt at the time that they held any power over their patients. This was true even of psychiatrists whose patients were vulnerable. They were flattered by their patient's attention. Many of these clinicians had grappled with personal problems of their own and had low self-esteem.

The doctor-ethicist Howard Brody, in his insightful

book *The Healer's Power* (1992), wrote that medical ethics is ultimately about power and its responsible use.[6] He identified a doctor's power as falling into three components: *aesculapian* power, arising by virtue of a doctor's training and knowledge of medicine; *charismatic* power, arising from a doctor's personal qualities such as kindness and firmness; and *social* power, arising from the high social status held by doctors.

The lesson here is that to use power responsibly, one must first recognise its existence. Doctors may have less social power today than they did for much of the 20th century, particularly in the Western world. In 2025, the easy availability of medical knowledge may have reduced the *aesculapian* element, but less power does not mean no power. It is still there, even in the age of AI.

In March 2023, I wrote in the British Medical Journal:

> *Only if doctors recognise their power can they begin to comprehend how it influences the doctor-patient relationship, how best to use it, how to control it, and how much of it to share with patients and colleagues.*[7]

6 Brody H, *The Healer's Power* (New Haven 1992)

7 Sokol D, 'The Power of Doctors' (2023) British Medical Journal 380: 498

LESSON 3

Clinicians must be scrupulously honest in and out of work

About 70% of the clinicians who attended the course had been accused of dishonest conduct. It is so common that the 'dishonesty' file on my computer contains eight sub-sections:

1. Cheating in exams
2. Defrauding the NHS
3. Dishonesty in job applications
4. Dishonesty in a non-medical context
5. Failure to disclose criminal offence to the regulator
6. Falsification of medical records
7. Falsification of other documents
8. Other types of dishonesty

Clinicians who have engaged in dishonesty are in a challenging position because dishonesty is difficult to cure. If a clinician has failed to insert a central line safely, for example, he or she can attend a course to master this skill, but what about the clinician whose failure is an act of dishonesty? There is a presumption that dishonest clinicians suffer from a character flaw that renders them untrustworthy and potentially unsuitable for practice, but that is not necessarily the case.

The philosopher Judith André has divided ethical behaviour into three stages: 1. moral perception (awareness that ethics is in play), 2. moral reasoning (working out, through reasoning, the morally right action), and 3. moral action (acting on the conclusion of your moral reasoning).[8]

Although ethical issues do not come pre-labelled (hence the frequent failures of moral perception), most of the attendees knew that they had acted dishonestly and hence in breach of an ethical rule. They usually faltered at the next stage: moral reasoning. In weighing up the pros and cons, they failed to ascribe sufficient weight to the wrongness of their deception,

8 Andre J, *Bioethics as Practice* (Chapel Hill 2002)

in particular the potential damage to trust.[9] They convinced themselves that their dishonesty, while technically a 'rule breach', was harmless and therefore justified, especially if no patients were directly affected.

The clinician who used a smartphone to check answers in a professional exam believed it was wrong but harmless. So too the doctor who made up internships to boost a CV, the doctor who falsely added FRCP (Fellow of the Royal College of Physicians) to his name, the doctor who left his NHS duties early to do private work, or the dentist who claimed NHS compensation for fictitious procedures. The dentist was investigated by the NHS Counter Fraud Authority, convicted of fraud by false representation, and narrowly avoided a custodial sentence in the Crown Court.

Only in hindsight did the clinicians realise that their actions were an abuse of trust, with potentially

9 Trust has been conceptualised in many ways. Johnson's Dictionary (1755) defines it as 'the firm belief in the reliability, truth or ability of someone or something (confidence, faith, belief)'. More recently, Michael Swash observed that 'trust is built on the mutual expression of confidence in the behaviour of others, relying on the competence, reliability, integrity, interpersonal relations and communication skills, not only between individuals, but between individuals and organisations.' Swash M, 'Trust in Healthcare' (2022) Journal of the Royal Society of Medicine 115(9): 360

adverse consequences for current patients or, at least, future patients. I ask them '*Who is less likely to trust you and your profession because of your actions, and why?*', and this prompts them to think about their patients, colleagues, regulators, the public, and any other parties whose trust they may have damaged.

The issue of dishonesty looms so large in my caseload that, with the assistance of a psychologist and six medically qualified professors of medical ethics, I developed an honesty test.[10] The test consists of 22 real-life scenarios, each with four possible answers. In each case, respondents are asked to select the best answer and the worst one. Below is an example, which you are invited to attempt.

10. Insurance

Your insurance covering your private practice ran out last week.

Later today, you will see a long-standing private patient for a simple but semi-urgent procedure. You will not be able to finalise the insurance arrangements before then as this may take weeks. The procedure is invasive but low risk.

Which answer do you consider the best and which the worst?

---

10 Sokol D, 'Developing an Honesty Test for Doctor' (2023) Journal of Medical Ethics Blog, URL: https://blogs.bmj.com/medical-ethics/2023/02/14/developing-an-honesty-test-for-doctors/ (accessed 28th March 2025)

1. Operate on the patient without insurance

2. Operate without insurance but exercising particular caution to minimise the risk to the patient

3. Do not treat the patient and recommend suitable colleagues who could perform the procedure

4. Inform the patient that you are *"finalising insurance arrangements"* and only operate if the patient consents to treatment after hearing your explanation

ANSWER	BEST	WORST
1.	☐	☐
2.	☐	☐
3.	☐	☐
4.	☐	☐

Option 1 is dishonest (and, in some jurisdictions, unlawful) as patients reasonably assume that their treating clinician is insured. It would be tragic if, in the event of negligence leading to serious harm, the patient was deprived of compensation because the clinician was uninsured or inadequately covered. In the UK, the General Medical Council expressly states in Rule 101 of Good Medical Practice: '*You must make sure that you have appropriate and adequate insurance or indemnity that covers the full scope of your practice. You should keep your level of cover under regular review.*'

Option 1 is the worst as it shows no appreciation of the risks of operating on a patient without insurance.

Option 2 remains dishonest, however cautious the clinician. In real life, this was the option selected by the doctor, who had declined to renew his insurance as he considered it too expensive.

Option 3 is the best. It is an honest and prudent response.

Option 4 provides an unclear explanation of the insurance situation and may leave the patient believing that insurance is in place.

I administer the test to the clinicians as an ethical training tool. Although a strong performance in the test does not guarantee honest conduct in practice, it at least shows a capacity to distinguish right from wrong in the domain of truth-telling.

The take-away message is that clinicians must act honestly in and out of work, whether it is to patients, colleagues, employers, insurers, or anyone else, and they must understand *why* this duty is so revered by their regulator.

The simple answer to the 'why' question is that dishonesty tends to erode trust, not only in the clinician but in the medical profession as a whole. If Howard Brody believes medical ethics is about the responsible use of power, the bioethicist Rosamond Rhodes contends that the core duty of medical ethics, from which all other duties are derived, is to seek trust and be deserving of that trust.[11] Regardless of whose theory is preferred, power and trust are central themes of the course.

---

11 Rhodes R, *The Trusted Doctor: Medical Ethics and Professionalism* (Oxford 2020)

LESSON 4

Seek help from others

A recurring regret among attendees is their failure to seek advice before making their ill-fated decision. In my opinion, getting help is the single most effective way to avoid serious errors of judgement.

If a colleague sought your advice and asked you *"I'm short of patient feedback forms for my appraisal. Shall I just make some up?"* or*"I'm attracted to one of my patients. Shall I ask them out on a date?"* or *"Shall I cheat in my exam?"*, how would you answer?

The clinicians on the course reached the wrong answer. Not a single one had sought the views of others. Had they done so, the friend or adviser would probably have pointed out blind spots, and flaws in reasoning, or at least brought a different perspective to the problem.

What emerges from all the cases is the value of friends or colleagues (or other 'support networks') who can be accessed easily in times of stress or difficulty.

In preparing this essay, I asked some past attendees who attended my course this question: '*Based on your experience, what is the most important piece of advice you would give a young doctor to avoid professional trouble?*'

One respondent, who was under investigation for inappropriately accessing a patient's medical records, echoed the advice of the doctor who was stopped for using his father's travel card but he stressed the importance of seeking help:

> *The public and society have high expectations of doctors. With this in mind, always stop and think before doing something. At least ask a trusted colleague to sense check you or tell you when you need to seek help and take a step back from a situation.*

Another respondent, a psychiatrist who started a sexual relationship with a patient, wrote:

> *Avoid professional isolation. Have regular mentoring and/or supervision, whatever grade you are - even consultant - with someone you feel provides a psychologically safe space.*

A third respondent, a general practitioner, was succinct: *'Pause. Don't panic. Get advice'*.

The advice to pause and seek help applies even after making an error. All too often, clinicians err in ways that would warrant only a minor sanction, only to turn a manageable situation into a far more serious one by attempting to cover up their wrongdoing. For instance, one doctor improperly took antibiotics from the hospital to treat his partner's chest infection. When confronted, instead of admitting the mistake, he tried to persuade colleagues to make up a cover story, compounding his original transgression to a new level of seriousness.

A similar situation arose with a dentist tasked with extracting a diseased tooth. Although she did so successfully, she also mistakenly removed a healthy one. Rather than inform the patient of the incident, she chose to say nothing. This decision to withhold the truth ultimately led to a referral to the General Dental Council. It brings to mind a saying popularised by the Canadian astronaut Chris Hadfield: '*There is no problem so bad that you can't make it worse.*'[12]

The biggest obstacle to getting help is ourselves. We may be overconfident, or too proud, or too ashamed to

---

12 Spector D, There's a Saying in the Space Business That Will Make You Rethink Risk (2014) Business Insider, 18th March 2014

ask others. We may see it as a sign of weakness rather than wisdom. We may fool ourselves into thinking that there is no time, or no need, to seek help, or that it is simply too tiring or complicated to do so.

In another BMJ column, I wrote:

> *If your ethical antennae pick up something troubling, however inchoate, or however confident you are that you can cope with it alone, ask someone else for their take on the situation. It may demand a few minutes of your time and theirs, and it may be embarrassing, but it could save you from a career ending blunder.*[13]

If in doubt, ask.

13 Sokol D, 'How to Avoid Bad Decisions That Can Ruin Your Career' (2024) British Medical Journal 386: 1584

LESSON 5

Medicine is not 'just a job'

In every course, I refer to the Declaration of Geneva. The Declaration was first adopted by the General Assembly of the World Medical Association in September 1948, shortly after the end of the Second World War. A year earlier, at the Nuremberg Tribunal, 20 Nazi doctors had been charged with murder, torture and atrocities committed in the name of medical science.

The Declaration contains the physician's pledge, which is sometimes described as a modern Hippocratic Oath. It contains vows such as '*I will respect the secrets that are confided in me, even after the patient has died*', *and* '*I will practise my profession with conscience and dignity and in accordance with good medical practice.*' A troubled conscience is a valuable warning sign. If it pricks, ask yourself how your actions might be judged in a court or tribunal.

The pledge underwent several modifications in subsequent years. The current version, amended in 2017, states that '*As a member of the medical profession...I will foster the honour and noble traditions of the medical profession*'.

An ethicist, who is a non-medical professor at a respected university, dismissed this as 'phenomenally pompous'. To him, being a doctor was 'just a job'.

After discussing the Oath and the Declaration, I ask clinicians on the course whether they agree with the professor: Do you believe that being a doctor (or dentist) is just a job?

So far, none have. Common answers are "*Being a doctor is part of who I am as a person*", "*It is a privilege to care for people*", "*It is a huge responsibility, with life and death consequences*", and "*Patients trust you not only with their bodies but with secrets which they tell no one else*". It is uplifting to hear these clinicians, in their moment of adversity, describe what being a doctor means to them.

Yet, morale among doctors in the UK is at a low ebb. Anecdotally at least, the work ethic and attitude of younger doctors differ from those of an older generation, aligning more closely with the professor's view that doctoring is a job like any other.

It would be a shame, I feel, for the medical profession to lose the sense that medicine is a profession like no other, in which head and heart combine to help a fellow human being in need, and that this commitment brings with it weighty moral obligations.

Some argue that today's clinicians face greater challenges than their predecessors. I am in no position to judge whether the role of the doctor in 2025 is more demanding than it was 50 or 100 years ago. Practising medicine in 1925, before the therapeutic revolution of the 1930s with sulfonamides and penicillin, would have been a rather bleak affair.

Lewis Thomas, a well-known American doctor who wrote eloquently about medicine, straddled the two eras. Before the 1930s, doctors could do little to prevent or cure disease. They could diagnose, explain, advise, relieve anxiety, and be with the patient at the time of death. Then everything changed. Lewis wrote:

> *Almost overnight, it became possible with antibiotics to cure outright some of the most common and lethal illnesses of human beings – lobar pneumonia, meningitis, typhoid, typhus, tuberculosis, septicemias of various types.* [...] *These events were simply overwhelming when they occurred.* [...] *I remember the earliest reaction of flat disbelief concerning such things. We had given up on therapy, a century earlier. With a few exceptions which we regarded as*

anomalies [...] *we were educated to be skeptical about the treatment of disease.*[14]

Today, medicine is infinitely more effective in diagnosing, prognosticating, preventing and curing disease. However, it is a victim of its success as people live longer, often with chronic conditions, and the health system cannot keep up with demand. The creaking system puts pressure on healthcare staff, who feel frustrated, exhausted, and undervalued.

While my emphasis in this essay is on the conduct of individual clinicians, it is plain that healthcare organisations have an important role to play in fostering an ethical culture, be it through their values, leadership, or business considerations. The interaction between institutional decision-making and ethical conduct is most stark in healthcare scandals affecting entire departments or hospitals, of which there are sadly too many, where the institution's leadership prioritise self-interest or reputation over patient care. An unhappy, dysfunctional or toxic clinical environment is hardly conducive to ethical conduct. Conversely, a clinician practising within an institutional culture which prizes a high standard of ethics, through its

14 Thomas L, *The Medusa and the Snail* (New York 1974)

policies, practices, and ethics training, is less likely to succumb to the temptation to act unethically. The institution, too, has an important role in encouraging ethical behaviour.

Two recurring themes in the writings of Sir William Osler remain relevant to doctors of all eras. They are, first, the inevitable obstacles that doctors will face in their lives, both personal and professional, and, second, the need to confront these with courage and an unwavering moral compass. In an address delivered in 1892, entitled 'Teacher and Student', Osler warned medical students that they would, at some stage, face a choice:

> *The choice lies open, the paths are plain before you. Always seek your own interests, make of a high and sacred calling a sordid business, regard your fellow creatures as so many tools of trade, and, if your heart's desire is for riches, they may be yours; but you will have bartered away the birthright of a noble heritage, traduced the physician's well-deserved title of the Friend of Man, and falsified the best traditions of an ancient and honourable Guild.*

If we can instill in students and clinicians a belief that their work is more than just a job, while preparing them as best we can - through regular teaching and role-modelling - to confront future challenges with courage and integrity, maybe fewer will take the wrong path.

The numbers who tread the wrong path are not trivial. For doctors alone, from 2020 to 2023, 936 doctors faced a Medical Practitioners Tribunal, with 229 erased from the GMC register and 353 suspended. Many more faced local disciplinary proceedings, which can also have a detrimental impact on mental health and career progression. All clinicians, however skilled or senior, should remain morally vigilant. As one attendee said, "*One mistake could cost you everything*".

CONCLUSION

In 1943, US General George Patton reputedly told his troops, "*It is an honour to die for your country. Make sure the other guy gets the honour.*"

The clinicians on my course have paid a heavy price for their errors, and their lessons.

My hope in this essay was to allow other clinicians - those who have so far steered clear of trouble - to learn some of these lessons vicariously, with only the pain of my company for an hour.

If I may restate them, the lessons are these: make ethics education a priority; be acutely aware of the power you hold and use it responsibly; be scrupulously honest in your dealings with patients, colleagues and others; develop and maintain a trusting group of friends and colleagues with whom you can discuss any problems; and always uphold the high moral standards of your profession, remembering that it is not 'just a job'.

I am grateful to the clinicians who attended my course for sharing their experiences, and to you for your attention.

INTRODUCING SIR WILLIAM OSLER

William Osler circa 1912
(in the public domain, source: Wikimedia Commons)

Shortly after Osler's death on 29th December 1919, the celebrated haematologist Richard Cabot wrote, '*I doubt if any single man has ever so deeply influenced any other profession*'.

Ten years later, Fielding Garrison, a physician-historian, called him '*the greatest physician of our time*'. More than a hundred years on, despite the enormous changes in medicine, Osler's influence remains strong.

Born in 1849 in Ontario, Canada, Osler studied medicine at McGill University. Following stints in London, Berlin and Vienna, he returned to teach at McGill and practised at the Montreal General Hospital. He was fascinated by pathology and reputedly conducted over 1000 autopsies. In 1884, he was appointed Professor of Clinical Medicine at the University of Pennsylvania, where he quickly gained a reputation as a first-class doctor and educator.

In 1889, Osler became the first professor of medicine at the newly formed Johns Hopkins University School of Medicine, where he taught alongside other giants of medicine: the pathologist William Welch, the surgeon William Halsted, and the gynaecologist Howard Kelly.

In 1892, Osler single-handedly wrote what became the leading medical textbook in the USA, Canada and the United Kingdom: *The Principles and Practice of Medicine*. The book went through 16 editions in 55 years. It only ceased publication in

1947, long after Osler's death.

His legacy also endures in the conditions that bear his name, such as Osler's nodes, Osler's disease (Osler-Vasquez disease, or polycythemia vera), and Osler's syndrome (Rendu-Osler-Weber syndrome, or hereditary haemorrhagic telangiectasia).

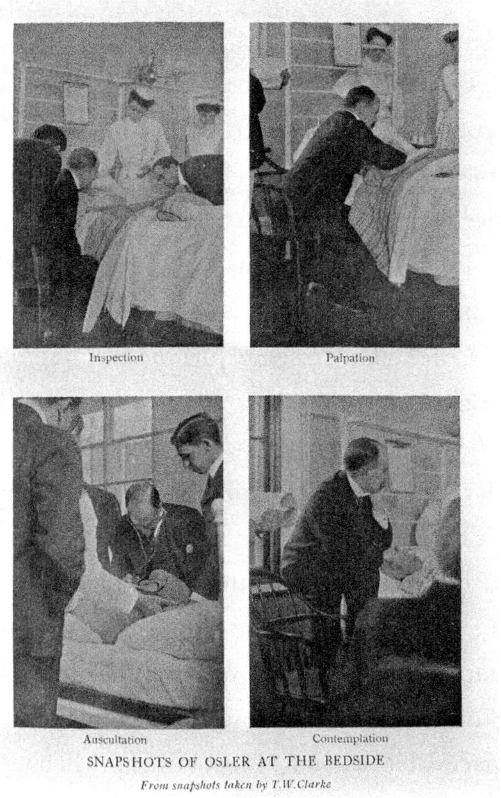

William Osler at the bedside
(Wellcome Collection. CC BY 4.0. Source: Wikimedia Commons)

In 1905, Osler moved to England, where he became Regius Professor of Medicine at Oxford University. By all accounts, he was blessed with a kind, generous, and friendly personality, with charm and wit in abundance. He made others feel at ease and was adored by all who met him. So welcoming was he to students and staff that his home at 13 Norham Gardens became known as the Open Arms. In 1911, Osler was made a baronet by King George V in recognition of his contributions to medicine and became 'Sir William'.

Osler was no stranger to tragedy. In 1917, his only child, Edward Revere, was killed on the battlefield in Flanders, Belgium. A grieving Osler wrote, '*The Fates do not allow the good fortune that has followed me to go with me to the grave - call no man happy until he dies.*'

Osler died on 29th December 1919 from complications of pneumonia, at the age of 70.

In 1925, Osler's friend and student, the great neurosurgeon Harvey Cushing, published a two-volume biography, *The Life of Sir William Osler*, which won the Pulitzer Prize. For those seeking a more modern and accessible account, I recommend Michael Bliss' *William Osler: A Life in Medicine* (1999).

The literature on Osler is vast, including dozens of books and thousands of articles on many facets of medicine, from pathology to infectious diseases. This is unsurprising given his status as one of the last 'super generalist' doctors.

There are Osler medical societies in several countries, including the American Osler Society, the Osler Club of London, the Chinese Osler Society, and the William Osler Society of Australia and New Zealand. These societies organise lectures and conferences on medical history and the humanities. Some medical schools also have Osler societies, the oldest of which may be at Western University in Ontario, Canada. Founded in 1925, it is still going strong. Their motto - 'Dare we dream' - comes from a speech by Osler to the British Medical Association in Montreal:

> *Distinctions of race, nationality, colour, and creed are unknown within the portals of the temple of Aesculapius* [ancient Greco-Roman god of medicine and healing]. *Dare we dream that this harmony and cohesion so rapidly developing in medicine, obliterating the strongest lines of division, knowing no tie of loyalty, but loyalty to truth – dare we hope, I say, that in the wider range of human affairs a similar solidarity may*

ultimately be reached?[15]

With violent conflicts in Ukraine, Myanmar, Gaza, the Sahel and elsewhere, and with certain world leaders driven chiefly by self-interest, the vision of solidarity in human affairs sadly remains an aspirational dream.

Although not a medical ethicist in the modern sense, Osler's humanistic approach to medicine had a profound influence on the ethical standards of frontline doctors. There are still doctors, usually more advanced in age, who will tell you how Osler's writings played an important part in their professional development.

In assembling this collection, I invited members of the Osler Club of London to share their favourite quotes and reflections on Osler's influence on their practice. A selection of responses appears below.

Sir Peter Rubin, Emeritus Professor of Medicine at Nottingham University and former Chair of the General Medical Council, chose '*Listen to the patient; he is telling you the diagnosis*'. He elaborated:

---

15 Osler W, 'British Medicine in Greater Britain,' in *Aequanimitas, With Other Addresses to Medical Students, Nurses and Practitioners of Medicine* (New York 1906)

When I was a medical student at Oxford, I had the good fortune to have as consecutive medical tutors two giants of medicine at the time: Sir George Pickering [who, like Osler, was Regius Professor and lived in 13 Norham Gardens] *and Professor Paul Beeson. Both were masters of the art of taking a history and I remember Pickering saying that if you can't put yourself in your patient's shoes and see the world as they see it, you've not taken a proper history.*

Throughout my career, I began my history with two questions they taught me to ask: "When was the last time you felt completely well?"; and "What was the first thing you noticed that wasn't right?". It is astonishing how often the answers - uncomplicated by the later development of further symptoms, treatment, and so on - pointed me in the direction of the diagnosis.

Mr Graham Kyle, an ophthalmologist who studied and practised in Glasgow, shared this quote from Osler's address at the opening of the Pathological Institute in Glasgow: '*There is no bubble so iridescent, or that travels so far, as that blown by a good teacher*'.[16]

Dr John Ward, a leading Osler scholar and general practitioner, offered, '*The great republic of medicine knows, and has known no national boundaries*'.[17]

Professor Raanan Gillon, Emeritus Professor of Medical Ethics at Imperial College and a general practitioner, valued Osler's references to '*the doctor's privilege of getting to know the huge variety of human behaviour and also to not taking ourselves too seriously*'.

Professor Terence Ryan, Emeritus Professor of Dermatology at Oxford University and curator of Osler's home at 13 Norham Gardens, noted that Osler's therapeutic power was friendship and chose this quote: '*It is an unpardonable mistake to go about among patients with a long face.*'[18]

Sir Mayur Lakhani, Former President of the Royal College of General Practitioners, focused on Osler's contribution to the development of academic medicine:

---

16 Osler W, 'The Pathological Institute of a General Hospital' (1911) The Glasgow Medical Journal 5: 321-333

17 Osler W, 'The Importance of Post-Graduate Study' (1900) The Lancet 2: 73-5

18 Osler W, 'The Student Life', in *Aequanimitas, With Other Addresses to Medical Students, Nurses and Practitioners of Medicine* (New York 1906)

> *I have been struck by Osler's work in creating so-called university hospitals, which combined teaching, research, and patient care. A vivid quote I remember is Osler saying, 'Let there be an invasion of hospitals by universities.' This quote encapsulates Osler's vision of integrating academic rigour and research into medicine, significantly influencing modern healthcare.*

Dr Sundy Papalois and Dr Zoe Papalois, both resident doctors in England, chose the quote: '*Medicine is the science of uncertainty, and the art of probability*'. They explained:

> *As young resident doctors, one of the most difficult challenges is managing uncertainty. By applying our skills, knowledge, experiences and help from seniors, we strive to identify, as Osler states, the most probable cause and diagnosis for patients' presentations and start appropriate management.*

Mr Tom Hennigan, a colorectal surgeon, praised the Oslerian principle that '*the good physician treats the disease; the great physician treats the patient who has the disease.*' He illustrated this with an example from his practice:

> *I once saw a woman as a third opinion. My colleagues had deemed surgery futile and advised that she should be left to die of sepsis. I saw something different. I believed that the patient was suffering from a stercoral perforation caused by severe constipation and that it was operable. Despite my colleagues' conviction that nothing could be done, we proceeded with the operation.*

Eighteen years later, Hennigan crossed paths with the patient again, alive and well: '*The patient gained at least 18 years of good life because I treated the patient, not just the disease.*'

The list could go on.

Osler played a significant role in my growth as a medical ethicist and even as a barrister. His emphasis on treating patients with patience, kindness and without judgement, standing up for principle and justice, applying the Golden Rule of Humanity ('*what you do not like when done to yourself, do not do to others*') and not letting '*the ceaseless panorama of suffering dull that fine edge of sympathy with which we started*' still resonates. So, too, does his focus on hard work, heeding the lessons of experience, and cultivating the heart just as much as the head. I try to apply those lessons - with variable success - in my practice.

In 2007, I provocatively wrote in the *British Medical Journal*:

> *I have long held the dangerous belief that William Osler's essays, judiciously used, could render teachers of medical ethics redundant. Virtually all the medical student needs for ethical behaviour is contained within them.*[19]

Wilder Penfield, another pioneering neurosurgeon influenced by Osler at Oxford, observed in 1949:

> *He belongs to medical students of all time, as Lincoln belongs to the common man everywhere, a man who grew to be what he wanted by dint of hard work, and in whose footsteps any undergraduate may dare to 'hope and dream' that he may follow.*[20]

For time-starved readers, I have curated a selection of Osler's quotes and aphorisms which seem to me of particular relevance to medical students and doctors at the start of their professional journey. In this task,

---

19 Sokol D, 'Aequanimitas' (2007) British Medical Journal 335:1049

20 Penfield W, 'Hero Worship' (1949) Archives of Internal Medicine 84: 104-9

I am indebted to the excellent collections of Bean, Silverman, Murray, and Bryan.[21]

The extracts are no substitute for reading the works in full, but they offer an accessible introduction. For those interested in exploring Osler's most famous essays, *A Way of Life and Other Addresses with Commentary and Annotations* (Durham and London, 2001), edited by S. Hinohara and H. Niki, is well worth reading.

As was customary at the time, Osler used masculine pronouns to refer to both men and women. I have left this unchanged for historical accuracy. Unlike many of his contemporaries, Osler was supportive of women becoming doctors. He wrote:

> *If any woman feels that the medical profession is her vocation, no obstacle should be placed in the way of her obtaining the best possible education, and every facility should be offered, so that, as a practitioner, she should have a fair start in the race.*

In an age where artificial intelligence and high-tech

---

21 Bean W (ed), Sir William Osler: *Aphorism From His Bedside Teaching and Writings* (New York 1850); Silverman M, Murray J and Bryan C, *The Quotable Osler* (Philadelphia, 2008)

medicine threaten to eclipse both the patient and the clinician, Osler's counsel to balance head and heart without losing sight of the human side of medicine seems more relevant than ever. I hope that these excerpts will provide some inspiration for your studies and your life.

Sketch of Sir William Osler by Dr Zoe Papalois, Neurosurgery Trainee

QUOTES FROM SIR WILLIAM OSLER FOR STUDENTS OF MEDICINE

Lifelong Learning and Education

1. 'It is a good many years since I sat on the benches, but I am happy to say that I am still a medical student, and still feel that I have much to learn.'

— Osler W, 'Address to the Students of the Albany Medical College' (1899) Albany Medical Annals 20: 307-9

2. 'Medicine is a most difficult art to acquire. All the college can do is to teach the student principles, based on facts in science, and give him good methods of work. These simply start him in the right direction; they do not make him a good practitioner - that is his own affair.'

— Osler W, 'Medicine and Nursing', in Mathews B (ed), *Essays on Vocation* (London 1919) 7

3. 'A great university has a dual function, to teach and to think.'

— Osler W, 'Teaching and Thinking', in *Aequanimitas, With Other Addresses to Medical Students, Nurses and Practitioners of Medicine* (New York 1906)

4. 'The hardest conviction to get into the mind of a beginner is that the education upon which he is engaged is not a college course, not a medical course, but a life course, for which the work of a few years under teachers is but a

preparation. Whether you will falter and fail in the race or whether you will be faithful to the end depends on the training before the start, and on your staying powers...You can all become good students, a few may become great students, and now and again one of you will be found who does easily and well what others cannot do at all, or very badly, which is John Ferriar's [Scottish physician] excellent definition of a genius.'

— Osler W, 'The Student Life', in *Aequanimitas, With Other Addresses to Medical Students, Nurses and Practitioners of Medicine* (New York 1906)

5. 'To study the phenomena of disease without books is to sail an uncharted sea, while to study books without patients is not to go to sea at all.'

— Osler W, 'Books and Men', in *Aequanimitas, With Other Addresses to Medical Students, Nurses and Practitioners of Medicine* (New York 1906)

6. 'The true student defies definition, but there are three unmistakable signs by which you can recognize the genuine article...an absorbing desire to know the truth, an unswerving steadfastness in its pursuit, and an open, honest heart, free from suspicion, guile, and jealousy.'

— Osler W, 'The Student Life', in Hinohara S, and Niki H, (eds) *A Way of Life and Other Addresses with Commentary and Annotations* (Durham and London 2001)

7. 'To an inquisitive mind the study of medicine may become an absorbing passion full of fascinating problems, so many of which present a deep human interest...It is hard indeed to name a dry subject in the curriculum. And yet in an audience of medical students such a statement nowadays raises a smile. Why? Because we make the examination the end of education, not an accessory in its acquisition.'

— Osler W, 'Examinations, Examiners and Examinees' (1913) The Lancet 182: 1047-50

8. 'Learn to love the freedom of the student life, only too quickly to pass away; the absence of the coarser cares of after days, the joy in comradeship, the delight in new work, the happiness in knowing that you are making progress. Once only can you enjoy these pleasures.'

— Osler W, 'The Master-Word in Medicine', in *Aequanimitas, With Other Addresses to Medical Students, Nurses and Practitioners of Medicine* (New York 1906)

9. 'As the practice of medicine is not a business and can never be one, the education of the heart - the moral side of man - must keep pace with the education of the head. Our fellow creatures cannot be dealt with as man deals with corn and coal; "the human heart by which we live" must control our professional relations.'

— Osler W, 'On the Educational Value of the Medical Society', in *Aequanimitas, With Other Addresses to Medical Students, Nurses and Practitioners of Medicine* (New York 1906)

10. 'Make the lesson of each case tell on your education. The value of experience is not in seeing much, but in seeing wisely.'

— Osler W, 'The Army Surgeon', in *Aequanimitas, With Other Addresses to Medical Students, Nurses and Practitioners of Medicine* (New York 1906)

11. 'To each of you, I would give the same advice. This feeling of disgust and weariness in study, this disheartening sense of want of progress, is natural; be prepared for it, meet it like a man; the mere effort will draw out the energy you hold in reserve, and you may find, perchance, as many a student has found before you, that the duties taken up with distaste become attractive in the doing of them.'

— Osler W, 'Introductory Lecture on the Opening of the Forty-Fifth Session of the Medical Faculty' (1877) Canada Medical and Surgical Journal 6: 193-210

12. 'I desire no other epitaph than the statement that I taught medical students in the wards, as I regard this as by far the most useful and important work I have been called upon to do.'

— Osler W, 'The Fixed Period', in *Aequanimitas, With Other Addresses to Medical Students, Nurses and Practitioners of Medicine* (New York 1906)

Observation and Clinical Practice

13. 'The whole art of medicine is in observation, as the old motto goes, but to educate the eye to see, the ear to hear and the finger to feel takes time, and to make a beginning, to start a man on the right path, is all that we can do.'

— Osler W, 'On the Need of a Radical Reform in Our Methods of Teaching Senior Students' (New York 1903) Medical News 82: 49-53

14. 'Get the patient in a good light. Use your five senses. We miss more by not seeing than we do by not knowing. Always examine the back. Observe, record, tabulate, communicate.'

— Roberts S, 'William Osler, Clinician-Teacher', in Abbott M (ed), 'Sir William Osler Memorial Number' (Montreal 1926) Bulletin XI of the International Association of Medical Museums and Journal of Technical Methods 432

15. 'I wish I had time to speak of the value of note-taking. You can do nothing as a student in practice without it. Carry a small notebook which will fit into your waistcoat pocket, and never ask a new patient a question without notebook and pencil in hand.'

— Osler W, 'The Student Life', in *Aequanimitas, With Other Addresses to Medical Students, Nurses and Practitioners of Medicine* (New York 1906)

16. 'Thoroughness is the most difficult habit to acquire, but it is the pearl of great price, worth all the worry and trouble of the search.'

— Osler W, 'The Student Life', in *Aequanimitas, With Other Addresses to Medical Students, Nurses and Practitioners of Medicine* (New York 1906)

17. 'Slow of growth, and the fruit of a seasoned experience, good clinical judgment only comes with careful study, and is best seen in men who appreciate the value of thoroughness in their work.'

— Osler W, *Modern Medicine, Its Theory and Practice* (Philadelphia 1907) 1: xv-xxxiv

18. 'To take a good history, to take one in a methodical manner, and last, but by no means the least, to put it down in a legible, attractive manner, takes careful training and much practice.'

— Osler W, 'The Natural Method of Teaching the Subject of Medicine' (1901) Journal of the American Medical Association 34: 191-197

19. 'The killing vice of the young doctor is intellectual laziness.'

— Osler W, 'On the Educational Value of the Medical Society', in *Aequanimitas, With Other Addresses to Medical Students, Nurses and Practitioners of Medicine* (New York 1906)

20. 'To carefully observe the phenomena of life in all its phases, normal and perverted, to make perfect that most difficult of all arts, the art of observation, to call to aid the science of experimentation, to cultivate the reasoning faculty, as to be able to know the true from the false - these are our methods. To prevent disease, to relieve suffering and to heal the sick - this is our work.'

— Osler W, 'Chauvinism in Medicine', in *Aequanimitas, With Other Addresses to Medical Students, Nurses and Practitioners of Medicine* (New York 1906)

21. 'Listen to the patient. He is telling you the diagnosis.'

— VanderVeer J, and Bryan CS, *Osler for White Coat Pockets* (2017) 102

22. 'A physician who treats himself has a fool for a patient.'

— Bean W (ed), *Sir William Osler: Aphorism From His Bedside Teaching and Writings* (New York 1850) 49

23. 'Care more particularly for the individual patient than for the special features of the disease.'

— Bean W (ed), *Sir William Osler: Aphorism From His Bedside Teaching and Writings* (New York 1850) 93

24. 'There is a tendency among young men about hospitals to study the cases, not the patients, and in the interest they take in the disease lose sight of the individual. Strive against this.'

— Gardner A, 'Some Recollections of Sir William Osler at Oxford' (1969) Journal of American Medical Association 210: 2265-7

25. 'Every patient you see is a lesson in much more than the malady from which he suffers.'

— Osler W, 'The Student Life', in *Aequanimitas, With Other Addresses to Medical Students, Nurses and Practitioners of Medicine* (New York 1906)

26. 'In my behavior to my patients I make no difference whatsoever between the high and the low, between a duchess and a cook.'

— Osler W, 'The Student Life', in *Aequanimitas, With Other Addresses to Medical Students, Nurses and Practitioners of Medicine* (New York 1906)

27. 'Medicine is learned by the bedside and not in the classroom. Let not your conceptions of the manifestations of disease come from words heard in the lecture room or read from the book. See, and then reason and compare and control. But see first...Live in the ward.'

— Thayer W, 'Osler the Teacher', in *Osler and Other Papers* (Baltimore 1931)

28. 'You will be glad to know that the training is in only three subjects - science, art, and the knowledge of men —Of equal importance one with another.'

— Osler W, 'The Reserves of Life' (1907) St Mary's Hospital Gazette 13: 95-98

29. 'Errors in judgment must occur in the practice of an art which consists largely in balancing probabilities.'

— Bean W (ed), *Sir William Osler: Aphorism From His Bedside Teaching and Writings* (New York 1850) 124

30. 'Gentlemen, if you want a profession in which everything is certain you had better give up medicine.'

—McRae T, 'The Influence of Pathology on the Clinical Medicine of William Osler', in Abbott M (ed), 'Sir William Osler Memorial Number' (Montreal 1926) Bulletin XI of the International Association of Medical Museums and Journal of Technical Methods 9

31. 'I have learned since to be a better student, and to be ready to say to my fellow students "I do not know".'

— Osler W, 'The Student Life', in *Aequanimitas, With Other Addresses to Medical Students, Nurses and Practitioners of Medicine* (New York 1906)

32. 'It is a common error to think that the more a doctor sees the greater his experience and the more he knows.'

— Bean W (ed), *Sir William Osler: Aphorism From His Bedside Teaching and Writings* (New York 1850) 48

33. 'Not only are the reactions of patients themselves variable, but we, the doctors, are so fallible, ever beset with the common and fatal facilities of reaching conclusions from superficial observations, and constantly misled by the ease with which our minds fall into the ruts of one or two experiences.'

— Osler W, 'Teacher and Student', in *Aequanimitas, With Other Addresses to Medical Students, Nurses and Practitioners of Medicine* (New York 1906)

Character and Virtues of a Physician

34. 'Mastery of self, conscientious devotion to duty, deep human interest in human beings - these best of all lessons you must learn now or never.'

— Osler W, 'Sir Thomas Browne', in *An Alabama Student* (New York 1909)

35. 'The physician needs a clear head and a kind heart; his work is arduous and complex, requiring the exercise of the very highest faculties of the mind, while constantly appealing to the emotions and finer feelings.'

— Osler W, 'Teaching and Thinking' in *Aequanimitas, With Other Addresses to Medical Students, Nurses and Practitioners of Medicine* (New York 1906)

36. 'Be careful when you get into practice to cultivate equally well your hearts and your heads.'

— Osler W, 'Address to the Students of the Albany Medical College' (1899) Albany Medical Annals 20: 307-9

37. 'If naturally devoid of the milk of human kindness, to assume a kindly interest in the sick is impossible. This was the meaning of that striking remark of Hippocrates that to a proper love of the profession must be joined a love for humanity —Or words to that effect.'

— Osler W, 'An Address on the Medical Clinic: A Retrospect and A Forecast' (1914) British Medical Journal 1(2766): 10-16

38. 'I have always felt that...we can all take a lesson from our French colleagues, whose gentle courtesy towards their patients has always made a deep impression upon me. In the wards of the Bicêtre, or of the Salpêtrière [two hospitals in Paris]...the greetings of the old men and women show how they feel that in their physician one friend at any rate is left.'

— Osler W, 'An Address on the Medical Clinic: A Retrospect and A Forecast' (1914) British Medical Journal 1(2766): 10-16

39. 'I have made mistakes, but they have been mistakes of the head not of the heart.'

— Osler W, 'L'Envoi', in *Aequanimitas, With Other Addresses to Medical Students, Nurses and Practitioners of Medicine* (New York 1906)

40. 'I have had three personal ideals. One to do the day's work well and not to bother about tomorrow...To it, more than anything else, I owe whatever success I have had - to this power of settling down to the day's work and

trying to do it well to the best of one's ability, and letting the future take care of itself. The second ideal has been to act the Golden Rule, as far as in me lay, toward my professional brethren and toward the patients committed to my care. And the third has been to cultivate such a measure of equanimity as would enable me to bear success with humility, the affection of my friends without pride, and to be ready when the day of sorrow and grief came to meet it with the courage befitting a man.'

— Osler W, 'L'Envoi', in *Aequanimitas, With Other Addresses to Medical Students, Nurses and Practitioners of Medicine* (New York 1906)

41. 'The quiet life in day-tight compartments will help you to bear your own and others' burdens with a light heart.'

— Osler W, 'The Student Life', in Hinohara S, and Niki H, (eds) *A Way of Life and Other Addresses with Commentary and Annotations* (Durham and London 2001)

42. 'To have striven, to have made an effort, to have been true to certain ideals - this alone is worth the struggle.'

— Osler W, 'Sir Thomas Browne', in *An Alabama Student* (New York 1909)

43. 'And, if the fight is for principle and justice, even when failure seems certain, where many have failed before, cling to your ideal.'

— Osler W, 'Aequanimitas', in *Aequanimitas, With Other Addresses to Medical Students, Nurses and Practitioners of Medicine* (New York 1906)

44. 'The word of action is stronger than the word of speech.'

— Osler W, 'Chauvinism in Medicine', in *Aequanimitas, With Other Addresses to Medical Students, Nurses and Practitioners of Medicine* (New York 1906)

45. 'And now, remembering that we have other duties towards you than teaching the details of your profession, I would on this occasion earnestly impress upon you the necessity of living upright, honest, and sober lives. The way of the medical student is beset with many temptations.'

— Osler W, 'Introductory Lecture on the Opening of the Forty-Fifth Session of the Medical Faculty, (1877) Canada Medical and Surgical Journal 6: 193-210

46. 'You are in this profession as a calling, not a business; as a calling which exacts from you at every turn self-sacrifice, devotion, love and tenderness to your fellow-men. Once you get down to a purely business level, your influence is gone and the true light of your life is dimmed. You must work in the missionary spirit, with a breadth of charity that raises you far above the petty jealousies of life.'

— Osler W, 'The Reserves of Life' (1907) St Mary's Hospital Gazette 13: 95-98

47. 'In the first place, in the physician or surgeon no quality takes rank with imperturbability...this essential bodily virtue...means coolness and presence of mind under all circumstances, calmness amid storm, clearness of judgment in moments of grave peril...In the second place, there is a mental equivalent to this bodily endowment, which is as important in our pilgrimage as imperturbability...a calm equanimity is the desirable attitude. How difficult to attain, yet how necessary, in success as in failure! Natural temperament has much to do with its development, but a clear knowledge of our relation to our fellow-creatures and to the work of life is also indispensable.'

— Osler W, 'Aequanimitas', in *Aequanimitas, With Other Addresses to Medical Students, Nurses and Practitioners of Medicine* (New York 1906)

Empathy, Compassion, and Patient Care

48. 'Medicine arose out of the primal sympathy of man with man; out of the desire to help those in sorrow, need and sickness.'

—Osler W, *The Evolution of Modern Medicine* (Yale University 1913)

49. 'Kindliness of disposition and gentleness of manners are qualities essential in a practitioner. If they do not exist naturally, they are virtues which must be cultivated if not assumed...The kindly word, the cheerful greeting, the sympathetic look, trivial though they may seem, help to brighten the paths of the poor sufferers and are often as 'oil and wine' to the bruised spirits entrusted to our care...remember that every patient ...will examine you critically and form an estimate of you by the way in which you conduct yourself at the bedside.'

— VanderVeer J and Bryan CS, *Osler for White Coat Pockets* (Masthof Press 2017) 21-22

50. 'In some of us the ceaseless panorama of suffering tends to dull that fine edge of sympathy with which we started...we physicians and nurses have but one enduring corrective - the practice towards patients of the Golden Rule of Humanity as announced by Confucius: 'What you do not like when done to yourself, do not do to others.'

— Osler W, 'Nurse and Patient', in *Aequanimitas, With Other Addresses to Medical Students, Nurses and Practitioners of Medicine* (New York 1906)

51. 'Nothing will sustain you more potently than the power to recognize in your humdrum routine, as perhaps it may be thought, the true poetry of life - the poetry of the commonplace, of the ordinary man, of the plain, toil-worn woman, with their love and their joys, their sorrows and their griefs.'

— Osler W, 'The Student Life', in *Aequanimitas, With Other Addresses to Medical Students, Nurses and Practitioners of Medicine* (New York 1906)

52. 'Once gain the confidence of a patient and inspire him with hope, and the battle is half won.'

— Osler W, 'The Reserves of Life' (1907) St Mary's Hospital Gazette 13: 95-98

53. 'In no relationship is the physician more often derelict than in his duty to himself.'

— Osler W, 'Dr Johnston as a Physician' (1902) Washington Medical Annals 1: 158-161

Professional Conduct and Ethics

54. 'If you cannot say anything good about a man, say nothing.'

— Pratt J, 'Osler as His Students Knew Him' (1920) Boston Medical Surgical Journal 182: 338-341

55. 'The wrangling and unseemly disputes which have too often disgraced our profession arise, in a great majority of cases, on the one hand, from this morbid sensitiveness to the confession of error, and, on the other, from a lack of brotherly consideration, and a convenient forgetfulness of our own failings.'

— Osler W, 'Teacher and Student', in *Aequanimitas, With Other Addresses to Medical Students, Nurses and Practitioners of Medicine* (New York 1906)

56. 'Shun as most pernicious that frame of mind, too often, I fear, seen in physicians, which assumes an air of superiority and limits as worthy of your communion only those with satisfactory collegiate or sartorial credentials. The passports to your fellowship should be honesty of purpose and a devotion to the highest interests of our profession.'

— Osler W, 'The Army Surgeon', in *Aequanimitas, With Other Addresses to Medical Students, Nurses and Practitioners of Medicine* (New York 1906)

57. 'Perhaps no sin so easily besets us as a sense of self-satisfied superiority to others. It cannot always be called pride, that master sin, but more often it is an attitude of mind which either leads to bigotry and prejudice or to such a vaunting conceit in the truth of one's own beliefs and positions, that there is no room for tolerance of ways and thoughts which are not as ours are.'

— Osler W, 'Chauvinism in Medicine', in *Aequanimitas, With Other Addresses to Medical Students, Nurses and Practitioners of Medicine* (New York 1906)

58. 'The trained nurse has become one of the great blessings of humanity, taking a place beside the physician and the priest, and not inferior to either in her mission.'

— Osler W, 'Nurse and Patient', in *Aequanimitas, With Other Addresses to Medical Students, Nurses and Practitioners of Medicine* (New York 1906)

59. 'Curious, odd compounds are these fellow-creatures, at whose mercy you will be; full of fads and eccentricities, of whims and fancies; but the more closely we study their little foibles of one sort and another in the inner life which we see, the more surely is the conviction borne upon us of the likeness of their weaknesses to our own.

The similarity would be intolerable, if a happy egotism did not often render us forgetful of it. Hence the need of an infinite patience and of an ever-tender charity toward these fellow-creatures; have they not to exercise the same toward us?'

— Osler W, 'Aequanimitas', in *Aequanimitas, With Other Addresses to Medical Students, Nurses and Practitioners of Medicine* (New York 1906)

60. 'One of the first essentials in securing a good-natured equanimity is not to expect too much of the people amongst whom you dwell...Deal gently then with this deliciously credulous old human nature in which we work, and restrain your indignation.'

— Osler W, 'Aequanimitas', in *Aequanimitas, With Other Addresses to Medical Students, Nurses and Practitioners of Medicine* (New York 1906)

Work Ethic and Fulfilment

61. 'Think not of the amount to be accomplished, the difficulties to be overcome, or the end to be attained, but set earnestly at the little task at your elbow, letting that be sufficient for the day.'

— Osler W, 'Introductory Lecture on the Opening of the Forty-Fifth Session of the Medical Faculty' (1877) Canada Medical and Surgical Journal 6: 193-210

62. 'The very first step towards success in any occupation is to become interested in it. Locke [philosopher and doctor] put this in a very happy way when he said, give a pupil "a relish of knowledge" and you put life into his work. And there is nothing more certain than that you cannot study well if you are not interested in your profession.'

— Osler W, 'The Student Life', in *Aequanimitas, With Other Addresses to Medical Students, Nurses and Practitioners of Medicine* (New York 1906)

63. 'I propose to tell you the secret of life as I have seen the game played and as I have tried to play it myself... Though a little one, the master-word looms large in meaning. It is the open sesame to every portal, the great equalizer in the world, the true philosopher's stone which transmutes all the base metal of humanity into gold. The stupid among you it will make bright, the bright

man brilliant, and the brilliant student steady. With the magic work in your heart all things are possible, and without it all study is vanity and vexation...True balm of hurt minds, in its presence the heart of the sorrowful is lightened and consoled. It is directly responsible for all advances in medicine during the past twenty-five centuries...The master-word is Work.'

— Osler W, 'The Master-Word', in *Aequanimitas, With Other Addresses to Medical Students, Nurses and Practitioners of Medicine* (New York 1906)

64. 'As to your method of work, I have a single bit of advice, which I give with the earnest conviction of its paramount influence in any success which may have attended my efforts in life - Take no thought for the morrow. Live neither in the past nor in the future, but let each day's work absorb your entire energies, and satisfy your widest ambition...The student who is worrying about his future, anxious over the examinations, doubting his fitness for the profession, is certain not to do so well as the man who cares for nothing but the matter in hand, and who knows not wither he is going!'

— Osler W, 'After Twenty-Five Years', in *Aequanimitas, With Other Addresses to Medical Students, Nurses and Practitioners of Medicine* (New York 1906)

65. 'Learn early to take the best possible care of the machine, never over-driving it, nor letting rust or dust collect in the bearings, and providing it with enough fuel to keep it going at a fair pace. Unlike any ordinary mechanism, the more you use it, the more, within limits, you can get out of it. Healthy action in a body out of which you can get plenty of work is the great asset in the race, the most important part, perhaps, of life's reserves.'

— Osler W, 'The Reserves of Life' (1907) St Mary's Hospital Gazette 13: 95-98

66. 'In ordinary training you run the course over, but life's race is run but once; and, though, the course may seem long to you, it is really very short, but very hard to learn. Fortunately, you are not alone on the track, as your brothers are ahead, and if you are willing there is always help at hand.'

— Osler W, 'The Reserves of Life' (1907) St Mary's Hospital Gazette 13: 95-98

67. 'You cannot get very far on the way until you have faith in your mission and your own relation to it. If you do not believe in yourself how can you expect other people to do so? If you have not an abiding faith in the profession you cannot be happy in it.'

— Osler W, 'The Reserves of Life' (1907) St Mary's Hospital Gazette 13: 95-98

Humility and Self-awareness

68. 'The Art of Detachment, the Virtue of Method, and the Quality of Thoroughness may make you students, in the true sense of the word, successful practitioners, or even great investigators; but your characters may still lack that which can alone give permanence to powers - the Grace of Humility. It may seem a little old-fashioned to preach the necessity of this virtue, but I insist for its own sake, and for the sake of what it brings, that a due humility should take the place of honour on the list.'

— Osler W, 'Teacher and Student', in *Aequanimitas, With Other Addresses to Medical Students, Nurses and Practitioners of Medicine* (New York 1906)

69. 'It takes courage to make a prognosis. Fulness of knowledge does not always bring confidence; the more one knows the more timidity may grow. The faculty which enables a man to look all round a question, to take a philosophical view of it, may be tempered with doubt, and an inability to reach a conclusion. A cocksure diagnosis and a positive prognosis may express the assurance of ignorance.'

— Osler W, 'The Lumleian Lectures on Angina Pectoris' (1910) The Lancet 1: 973-7

70. 'Keep a looking glass in your own heart, and the more carefully you scan your own frailties, the more tender you are for those of your fellow creatures.'

— Holman E, 'Sir William Osler: Teacher and Bibliophile' (1969) Journal of the American Medical Association 210: 2223-5

71. 'By far the most dangerous foe we have to fight is apathy - indifference from whatever cause, not from lack of knowledge, but from carelessness, from absorption in other pursuits, from a contempt bred of self-satisfaction.'

— Osler W, 'Unity, Peace and Concord', in *Aequanimitas, With Other Addresses to Medical Students, Nurses and Practitioners of Medicine* (New York 1906)

72. 'Every day do some reading or work apart from your profession. I fully realize, no one more so, how absorbing is the profession of medicine...but you will be a better man and not a worse practitioner for an avocation. I care not what it may be: gardening or farming, literature or history or bibliography.'

— Osler W, 'The Student Life', in *Aequanimitas, With Other Addresses to Medical Students, Nurses and Practitioners of Medicine* (New York 1906)

Philosophy and Perspective on Medicine

73. 'You enter a noble heritage, made so by no efforts of your own, but by the generations of men who have unselfishly sought to do the best they could for suffering mankind. Much has been done, much remains to do.'

— Osler W, 'The Master-Word in Medicine', in *Aequanimitas, With Other Addresses to Medical Students, Nurses and Practitioners of Medicine* (New York 1906)

74. 'Never lose sight of the end and object of all your studies; the cure of disease and the alleviation of suffering.'

— Osler W, 'Introductory Lecture on the Opening of the Forty-Fifth Session of the Medical Faculty' (1877) Canada Medical and Surgical Journal 6: 193-210

75. 'You have of course entered the Profession of Medicine with a view of obtaining a livelihood; but in dealing with your patients let this always be a secondary consideration.'

— Osler W, 'Valedictory Address to the Graduates in Medicine and Surgery, McGill University' (1874-5) Canada Medical and Surgical Journal 3: 433-442

76. 'Distinctions of race, nationality, colour and creed are unknown within the portals of the temple of Aesculapius [ancient Greco-Roman god of medicine and healing].'

— Osler W, 'British Medicine in Greater Britain', in *Aequanimitas, With Other Addresses to Medical Students, Nurses and Practitioners of Medicine* (New York 1906)

77. 'The all-important matter is to get a breadth of view as early as possible, and this is difficult without travel.'

— Bean W (ed), *Sir William Osler: Aphorism From His Bedside Teaching and Writings* (New York 1850) 79

78. 'In no profession does culture count for so much as in medicine, and no man needs it more than the general practitioner.'

— Bean W (ed), *Sir William Osler: Aphorism From His Bedside Teaching and Writings* (New York 1850) 52

79. 'The pulse of every student should beat faster as he reads the story of Archimedes, of Hero, of Aristarchus - names not even mentioned in the 'Greats' papers [formal examinations at Oxford University] in the past decade. Yet the methods of these men exorcized vagaries and superstitions from the human mind and pointed to a clear knowledge of the laws of Nature.'

— Osler W, 'The Old Humanities and the New Science' (1919) British Medical Journal 2: 1-7

Challenges and Realities of Medicine

80. 'The greater the ignorance the greater the dogmatism'.

— Bean W, (ed), *Sir William Osler: Aphorism From His Bedside Teaching and Writings* (New York 1850) 88

81. 'The philosophies of one age have become the absurdities of the next, and the foolishness of yesterday has become the wisdom of tomorrow.'

— Bean W (ed), *Sir William Osler: Aphorism From His Bedside Teaching and Writings* (New York 1850) 88

82. 'In the progress of knowledge each generation has a double labour - to escape from the intellectual thralls of the one from which it has emerged and to forge anew its own fetters.'

— Osler W, 'The Treatment of Disease' (1909) Canada Lancet 42: 899-912

83. 'Hurry? Never hurry - hurry is the devil. More people are killed by hurry than by disease.'

— Osborne M, 'Recollections of Sir William Osler', in Abbott M (ed), 'Sir William Osler Memorial Number' (Montreal, 1926) Bulletin XI of the International Association of Medical Museums and Journal of Technical Methods

84. 'Punctuality is the prime essential of a physician - if invariably on time he will succeed even in the face of professional mediocrity.'

— Holman E, 'Sir William Osler: Teacher and Bibliophile' (1969) Journal of the American Medical Association 210: 2223-5

85. 'My message is chiefly to you, Students of Medicine, since with the ideals entertained now your future is indissolubly bound. The choice lies open, the paths are plain before you. Always seek your own interests, make of a high and sacred calling a sordid business, regard your fellow creatures as so many tools of trade, and, if your heart's desire is for riches, they may be yours; but you will have bartered away the birthright of a noble heritage, traduced the physician's well-deserved title of the Friend of Man, and falsified the best traditions of an ancient and honourable Guild.'

— Osler W, 'Teacher and Student', in *Aequanimitas, With Other Addresses to Medical Students, Nurses and Practitioners of Medicine* (New York 1906)

86. 'To each one of you the practice of medicine will be very much as you make it - to one a worry, a care, a perpetual annoyance; to another, a daily joy and a life of as much happiness and usefulness as can well fall to the lot of man.'

— Osler W, 'The Student Life', in *Aequanimitas, With Other Addresses to Medical Students, Nurses and Practitioners of Medicine* (New York 1906)

Wisdom and Practical Advice

87. 'Practically, there should be for each of you a busy, useful, and happy life; more you cannot expect; a greater blessing the world cannot bestow. Busy you will certainly be, as the demand is great...Useful your lives must be, as you will care for those who cannot care for themselves... And happy lives shall be yours, because busy and useful; having been initiated into the great secret - that happiness lies in the absorption in some vocation which satisfies the soul; that we are here to add what we can to, not to get what we can from, life.'

— Osler W, 'Doctor and Nurse', in *Aequanimitas, With Other Addresses to Medical Students, Nurses and Practitioners of Medicine* (New York 1906)

88. 'I started in life - I may as well own up and admit - with just an ordinary everyday stock of brains. In my schooldays I was much more bent upon mischief than upon books - I say it with regret now - but as soon as I got interested in medicine I had only a single idea and I do believe that if I have had any measure of success at all, it has been solely because of doing the day's work well that was before me just as faithfully and honestly and energetically as was in my power.'

— Cushing H, *The Life of Sir William Osler* (Oxford 1925)

89. 'What we call sense or wisdom is knowledge, ready for use, made effective, and bears the same relation to knowledge itself that bread does to wheat.'

— Osler W, 'The Student Life', in *Aequanimitas, With Other Addresses to Medical Students, Nurses and Practitioners of Medicine* (New York 1906)

90. 'To know just what has to be done, then to do it, comprises the whole philosophy of practical life.'

— Osler W, 'British Medicine in Greater Britain', in *Aequanimitas, With Other Addresses to Medical Students, Nurses and Practitioners of Medicine* (New York 1906)

91. 'Go out among your fellows, and learn of them.'

— Bean W (ed), *Sir William Osler: Aphorism From His Bedside Teaching and Writings* (New York 1850) 65

92. 'It helps a man immensely to be a bit of a hero-worshipper, and the stories of the lives of the masters of medicine do much to stimulate our ambition and rouse our sympathies.'

— Osler W, 'Chauvinism in Medicine', in *Aequanimitas, With Other Addresses to Medical Students, Nurses and Practitioners of Medicine* (New York 1906)

93. 'Familiarize yourself with the work of others and never fail to give credit to the precursor.'

— Bean W (ed), *Sir William Osler: Aphorism From His Bedside Teaching and Writings* (New York, 1850) 67

94. 'You cannot afford to stand aloof from your professional colleagues in any place. Join their associations, mingle in their meetings, giving of the best of your talents, gathering here, scattering there; but everywhere showing that you are at all times faithful students, as willing to teach as to be taught.'

— Osler W, 'The Student Life', in *Aequanimitas, With Other Addresses to Medical Students, Nurses and Practitioners of Medicine* (New York 1906)

95. 'The comedy, too, of life will be spread before you... the humorous side is really almost as frequently turned towards him [the doctor] as the tragic. Hilarity and good humour, a breezy cheerfulness, a nature "sloping towards the southern side" [a sunny disposition]...help enormously both in the study and in the practice of medicine. To many of a sombre and sour disposition it is hard to maintain good spirits amid the trials and tribulations of the day, and yet it is an unpardonable mistake to go about among patients with a long face.'

— Osler W, 'The Student Life', in *Aequanimitas, With Other Addresses to Medical Students, Nurses and Practitioners of Medicine* (New York 1906)

96. 'Like song that sweetens toil, laughter brightens the road of life, and to be born with a sense of the comic is a precious heritage.'

— Osler W, 'Two Frenchmen on Laughter', in 'Men and Books' (1912) Canadian Medical Association Journal 2: 152

97. 'Courage and cheerfulness will not only carry you over the rough places of life, but will enable you to bring comfort and help to the weak-hearted and will console you in the sad hours when, like Uncle Toby [a character from Laurence Sterne's The Life and Opinions of Tristram Shandy], you have 'to whistle that you may not weep'.

— Osler W, 'The Master-Word', in *Aequanimitas, With Other Addresses to Medical Students, Nurses and Practitioners of Medicine* (New York 1906)

98. 'But whatever you do, take neither yourselves nor your fellow-creatures too seriously. There is tragedy enough in our daily routine, but there is room too for a keen sense of the absurdities and incongruities of life, and in

the shifting panorama no one sees better than the doctor the perennial sameness of men's ways.'

— Osler W, 'The Reserves of Life' (1907) St Mary's Hospital Gazette 13: 95-98

99. 'The practitioner is frequently consulted for foul breath, and is daily made aware of its wide-spread prevalence. Too often he is himself the subject of the condition, to the disgust of his patients, with whom he has to come into such close contact.'

— Osler W, *The Principles and Practice of Medicine* (New York 1901) 439

100. 'In the life of a young man the most essential thing for happiness is the gift of friendship.'

— Bean W (ed), *Sir William Osler: Aphorism From His Bedside Teaching and Writings* (New York 1850) 31

ABOUT THE AUTHOR

The author delivering a lecture at the All India Institute of Medical Sciences, Jammu (India), August 2024

Daniel Sokol is a medical ethicist and barrister who practises law from chambers at 12 King's Bench Walk, London. He completed his undergraduate studies at the University of Oxford, followed by a master's and PhD in medical ethics at Imperial College London. As an academic, he taught medical ethics around the world, including the UK, USA, Australia, New Zealand, India, and Hong Kong.

Daniel has served on various committees, including for the UK Ministry of Defence, the Ministry of Justice, and the Royal College of Surgeons of England. He has also worked as a bioethics consultant for diverse organisations, from hospitals to theatres. Currently, he is Chairman of the Metropolitan Police Research Ethics Committee and President of the Osler Club of London.

In his legal practice, Daniel specialises in the fields of clinical negligence, personal injury, and education law, acting for both claimants and defendants. He is ranked as a leading lawyer in both The Legal 500 and Chambers and Partners. A regular columnist for the British Medical Journal, Daniel has published widely on law and ethics, *including Tough Choices: Stories from the Front Line of Medical Ethics* (2018) and, with Ronald Sokol, *A Young Person's Guide to Law and Justice* (2024).

ACKNOWLEDGEMENTS

This short book owes its existence to the generosity of the Dr Prem Nath Berry Educational Trust. Founded in 1962 by Dr Prem Nath Berry, the Trust has supported the advancement of public education and medical training in India. I am particularly grateful to Mr Harjeet Singh and the trustees for their encouragement and support, not only in bringing this project to fruition but also during previous visits to the impressive All India Institute of Medical Sciences in Vijaypur, Jammu and Kashmir, India.

I am also indebted to those who have kindly reviewed and improved drafts of the essay, in particular Alexander Fairbairn, Ronald Sokol, Chris McManus, Raanan Gillon, Greg Moorlock and Dita Wickins-Drazilova. Any errors that have somehow passed their fine filter are mine alone.

The essay was enriched by the comments of clinicians who attended my remedial ethics course, and I am most grateful for their thoughts and experiences.

The section on Osler has benefitted from the contributions of doctors and medical students who are members of that wonderful medical society, the Osler Club of London. These are Peter Rubin, Graham Kyle,

John Ward, Raanan Gillon, Terence Ryan, Mayur Lakhani, Tom Hennigan, Sunday Papalois, and Zoe Papolois. Zoe, a gifted artist, generously offered the sketch of Osler featured in that section.

I am especially thankful to Charles S. Bryan, Heyward Gibbes Distinguished Professor of Internal Medicine Emeritus at the University of South Carolina, Columbia, for his insightful foreword. I have long admired his scholarship on Osler and the medical humanities, and it is an honour to include his perspective in this work.

Finally, a special debt of gratitude to my wife, Samantha Hettige, and my two children, Ella and Nicholas, for their patience and understanding during the many hours I devoted to this project.

Thank you all for your support and inspiration.

Printed in Dunstable, United Kingdom

68402656R00068